A

Daily Dose

of

Yiddish

Barbara Rogers Jolovitz

A Daily Dose of Yiddish

ISBN 978-1-943424-69-6

LCCN 2021943447

North Country Press
Unity, Maine

"In a figurative way, Yiddish is the wise and humble language of us all, the idiom of a frightened and hopeful humanity."

—Isaac Bashevis Singer, 1978 Nobel Prize Winner for Literature

DEDICATION

To mein kinderlach who get a daily dose of Yiddish, to those who have had Yiddish in their lives and remember, and to those who are curious about Yiddish, *A Daily Dose of Yiddish* is dedicated to you. Zei gezunt und zei mir frailich. Be well and be happy.

INTRODUCTION

"Zei gezunt und zei mir frailich, mein ziskeit. Be well and be happy, my sweet. Zayde and I love you."

Bubbe.

Several years ago, I started sending grandsons Ben (now 28), Will (25), and Nicky (22) a daily email for the sole purpose of letting them know I was thinking of them and loved them. The email closed with the above. It was important to me they be reminded of their heritage and a Yiddish closing was the way to do it. Zayde had died but he was still very much alive in our hearts and I saw no reason to stop sending them his love.

After a while, in addition to the daily greeting, I started sending a Yiddish word or phrase with pronunciation and definition. I told a few people about the daily Yiddish and they, too, wanted a dose. They told their friends and their friends wanted Yiddish. A "class" was born and as of this writing (June 2020), there are 52 getting a daily dose of Yiddish. Many are not Jewish and I do not know everyone; however, everyone takes it seriously and will sometimes ask if I have a Yiddish word for something on their minds. "Zei gezunt und zei mir frailich, mein kinderlach. Be well and be happy, my children," ends the daily dose of Yiddish.

BUBBE'S WORLD

Learning we were to be grandparents, Lester and I talked about what we would like to have our grandchild call us. In our den are oval framed photographs of Lester's Bubbe and Zayde (Yiddish for grandmother and grandfather) taken in the late 1800s in their Ivye, Lithuania shtetl. Gray-bearded Zayde is wearing a wide-lapelled black jacket, white shirt, black tie, and resting mid-forehead is a fez-shaped fabric hat perhaps six inches high. Bubbe is wearing a sheitel, or wig, which married Jewish women wore and continue to wear in some Jewish communities. Her dress is black with a high fringed neck edged in white; she is wearing drop earrings with gemstones, a bar pin and a gold chain necklace with a pendant. Lester never knew his grandparents, but he felt akin to them and would say "my Bubbe told me" this or "my Zayde told me" that. Because of the pleasure we had from Zayde and Bubbe living with us, albeit in photographs, we would be Zayde and Bubbe to this eagerly awaited grandchild.

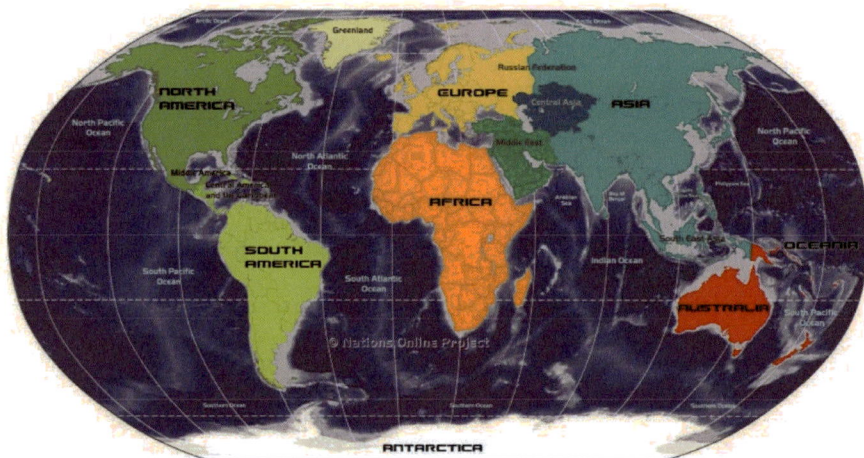

Bubbe's World

And, there is Bubbe's World. Lester was involved with the local YMCA and 51 years ago, he and two other men founded Camp Tracy, a YMCA summer camp for children. In more recent years, the Boys and Girls Clubs joined with the YMCA under the umbrella of the Alfond Youth Center, now known as the Alfond Youth & Community Center (AYCC). Ken Walsh came on the scene as its CEO and he and Lester became friends. Ken would come for lunch: BLINTZES with blueberry sauce. A new world opened up to him. His children, Sean and Kate, would call us Bubbe and Zayde. After Lester's death, I told Ken I would be pleased if he would like to call me Bubbe. Not too long after that, he and his associate Felicia, who was calling me Bubbe, came to the door wearing T-shirts printed with worlds and "Bubbe's World" lettering. Bubbe's World was born. Many in the Yiddish class call me Bubbe.

Yiddish originated around 1000 CE in Romance-speaking territories in what is now Southern France and Northern Italy. Jews began emigrating to the Middle Rhine Basin which included Southern and Western Germany and they took their Yiddish with them. Around the 12th Century, Yiddish was called "lashon ashkenaz," language of the Ashkenaz. It was also called mame-loshn, mother tongue. Mame-loshn means Yiddish and that term is used to this day.

Jews were given the "Yiddish" designation in the late 18th and into the 20th Century when mostly Eastern European immigrants started arriving in America where its streets were paved with gold: Di Goldene Medina - the Golden Land. Their names got changed at Ellis Island: my grandfather left Poland as Sklar and left Ellis Island as Goldberg; Lester's father left Lithuania as Yachvalovitz and left Ellis Island as Jolovitz. Yiddish, the common language, enabled the immigrants to communicate with each other. Many settled in Brooklyn and the Lower East Side of Manhattan. Women worked in sweat factories and men became peddlers. They brought their violins, their clarinets, flutes, percussion instruments, and brass horns: KLEZMER, traditional Eastern European Jewish music, had come to America. They wrote lyrics and music for Yiddish theater and performed in the shows; they wrote lyrics and music for Broadway productions and performed there as well. Babka, bagel and bialy bakeries opened. In 1897, they published their own Yiddish newspaper, the *Jewish Daily Forward*, recently out of print but available digitally.

Many moved away from New York where their peddling morphed into stores; they married, they spoke Yiddish at home, they learned some English and made sure their children were educated. They made America their Goldene Medina.

Before World War II, there were an estimated 10,690,000 Yiddish-speaking people throughout the world. By the 1900s, there were an estimated 1.5 to 2 million. Approximately 85% of the 6 million Jews who died in the Holocaust spoke Yiddish. In the 21st Century, it is estimated between 500,000 and 1,000,000 speak Yiddish, mainly in the United States, Canada, Europe and Israel. Hasidim and other Orthodox Jews speak Yiddish in their daily lives.

BLINTZES

Barbara's Blintzes

My mother defined blintzes as "the last hideout for **FARSCHIMMELT** (FarSCHIMmelt) —rotten cheese." She scoured the back of her refrigerator for bits of cottage cheese and cream cheese which when blended with an egg and a pinch of sugar would find its way into pancakes and magically become blintzes. The old strawberries she found got sliced up, sugared and spooned on the blintzes. The blintzes were dessert so there were just enough for the five of us. They were always a treat and **GESHMAK**-delicious.

It is hard to imagine making blintzes without a mixer for the filling, no blender for the batter, and no non-stick pan so the pancake didn't stick. Making them was, and is, a production. Once the cheese and batter are prepared comes putting them together to make the blintzes. Lightly coat a heated 10-inch pan with vegetable oil and pour in 1/4 cup of batter, rolling it around the bottom of the pan as in making crèpe. When the edge of the pancake is browned, run a knife around it and flip it on a dish towel placed on a hard surface. The cooked side of the pancake gets the cheese. Make another pancake and while it is cooking, the waiting pancake has 3 T. of cheese placed near the bottom; the bottom is then folded over the cheese, followed by the sides folded in, rolled up and set aside. You now have a blintz.

Unlike my mother's blintzes, mine start with a couple of pounds of Farmers Cheese or Ricotta, half a pound of cream cheese, 3 eggs, 3 T. sugar, zest of 1 lemon and 1/4 c. butter, melted, beaten together in a mixer. The pancake batter is made in a blender: 6 eggs, 1 1/2 c. flour, 1 tsp. salt, 1 1/2 c. milk, 1 1/2 c. water, 3 T. butter, melted. (Divide the batter in half if you have an old blender.) The production remains the same.

BLINTZ / noun

A pancake filled with a cheese mixture, rolled up, fried in butter, plated and served. They can be covered with a sauce of blueberries or strawberries and served with sour cream.

Blintzes are thought to have originated in Central Europe (Hungary, Poland, Slovenia) and that general area. Although they were probably around for hundreds of years, they gained popularity in the 1800s and came to America as blintzes, their Yiddish name.

BLINTZ / verb

To invite people to gather in your kitchen to create friendships and eat blintzes with blueberry sauce.

My kitchen has become a gathering place where friendships are created eating BLINTZES with blueberry sauce. Ken Walsh continued to come for blintzes after Lester's death. Ken told me he would like to bring people over to meet me and have blintzes. We would BLINTZ people. Blintz became a verb and blintzes were a new experience with few exceptions.

10

Ken had been helping to establish YMCAs among Native American tribes in Maine and met Chief Barry Dana who had been Chief of the Penobscot Nation in Old Town, Maine. Chief Dana also led a Native American Wilderness survival week at Camp Tracy. Ken invited Chief Dana for blintzes. I told Chief Dana I had been to Indian Island as a child as my grandparents lived in Bangor. I remembered being rowed over to the Island. Chief Dana told me his grandfather would have rowed us over.

District Attorney Maeghan Maloney on the Board of the AYC was blintzed. We shared stories about Lester's days as an attorney, including a commendation he had received from the Judge on a case Lester and his partner had defended, a case they knew they could not win.

There is a 2/3 replica of Fenway Park at YMCA Camp Tracy where two sessions of baseball camp are held each summer. The first session starts with baseball legends coaching the campers. Ken asked me to come to Fenway to meet Mike Torrez and Bucky Dent who shared a Red Sox -Yankees debacle (for the Red Sox) years ago. Another time, Mike Torrez and Luis Tiant came for the camp opening. We blintzed them. In 2017, a 2/3 replica of Chicago's Wrigley Field opened in Waterville. Fergie Jenkins, who played for the Cubs and is in the National Baseball Hall of Fame, served as Honorary Chair at the opening of Purnell Wrigley Field. Fergie enjoyed the blintzes immensely.

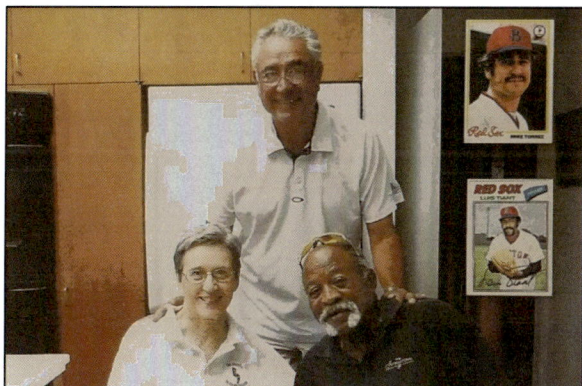

Barbara, Mike Torrez, Luis Tiant

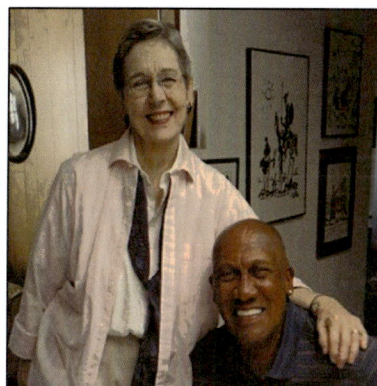

Barbara and Fergie Jenkins

11

ALLEN ISLAND

Herring Gut Learning Center was founded in 1997 by Phyllis Wyeth as a non-profit marine education center in Port Clyde, Maine. Nancy Baker, one of its recent Chair of the Board of Trustees, attended a conference at Colby College on environmental issues and greenhouses. The Alfond Youth Center was in the process of setting up a greenhouse and Ken attended the meeting. Nancy invited Ken to visit Herring Gut and was asked to join their Board. Knowing Nancy was coming to the AYC, Ken invited her to be blintzed. A gifted artist, Nancy shared one of her Maine scene paintings with me.

In August, 2018, there was a fundraising event at Wyeth's Allen Island for the Wyeth Family's Up East Foundation. Ken asked if I would like to attend. He was unable to go on the day of the event so his associate Felicia went in his stead. We would be ferried by lobster boat the half hour it took from Port Clyde to Allen Island. Jamie Wyeth greeted the guests and gave a tour of his museum; lunch was served and we were returned to Port Clyde. The tide was unusually low at 12 1/2 ft. so I had to "**SHLEP**" (haul) myself up a steep ramp to get on land where I was greeted by, "You're Barbara, aren't you? I understand you make blintzes." "Do you know what blintzes are?" "My grandmothers lived in New York and one had a pushcart." That encounter was with Peter Harris, Chair of the Board of Trustees of Herring Gut and recently on the Board of the Alfond Youth Center. Blintzing Peter was especially meaningful.

Covid-19 has interfered with blintzing but I made some for Ken with instructions for cooking at home. Peter has some waiting for him without cooking instructions.

Jamie Wyeth Museum

YIDDISH IN ODESSA

We met Beverly and Howard Moeckler 26 years ago in Naples, Florida. They are from Milwaukee and now at 92, they have forsaken Florida to stay in Milwaukee to be near their children. Beverly encouraged me to write nine years ago when I related a story to her and she said things like that don't happen in Milwaukee and I should write it down. *Reminiscences and Recipes* was the result. The following is from Beverly:

"Because my 'Grandpa' lived with our family after his wife died, I heard Yiddish spoken. Grandpa understood English but always answered in Yiddish. It's been many years since I have been exposed to those words and phrases, but I still remember most of them so fondly.

During the '70s, Howard and I took a cruise on a Russian freighter with stops in Odessa and Kyev (Kiev). One of our objectives was to visit a functioning synagogue. Unfortunately, the few we saw were locked.

We decided to walk around the synagogue block, speaking basic Yiddish to each other. Lo and behold the **SHAMMES** (caretaker) of the **SHUL** (synagogue) heard us. We conversed in Yiddish, he let us in his shul and gave us a tour of his old, well-used house of prayer. I will never forget."

KAIN EIN HOREH: (Kain ein HOReh). No evil eye; may nothing bad (evil) happen to you. (Lit. May no evil befall.)

The "evil eye" superstition appears in Jewish, Christian, Islamic, Hindu and Buddhist cultures. It is mentioned in Hebrew and Greek Bibles and remains a superstition to this day. "KAIN EIN HOREH" is said as one word: KAIneHOReh. It is equivalent to knocking on wood or any other gesture used to ward off something evil. My Greek friend Sophie used to make a spitting noise three times. You give a kainehoreh after **K'VELLING** (boasting with pride) over something.

Knocking on wood goes back to early believers who felt spirits lived in trees and by knocking on wood, you could alert them to help you. Jewish knocking on wood goes back to the Inquisition when Jews gave a coded knock on a wooden synagogue door in order to enter safely.

———————————

SOME YIDDISH C's

CHAZZER: (CHAzzer). Pig. Or, someone who wants more than what he needs. Or, someone who can be described as a messy eater or glutton. Jews are not supposed to eat pig (pork). Leviticus 11:7-8 instructed only an animal that has a split cloven hoof and chews its cud were Jews allowed to eat. Deuteronomy 14:3-6 said the same thing, adding their carcass shouldn't be touched either. Pigs have split cloven hoofs but do not chew their cud. Ox, lamb, ibex, giraffe and deer have split cloven hooves and chew their cuds. Edible.

CHAZZEREI: (CHAzeREI). Can be garbage, junk food, trash, shoddy merchandise; stuff of little value. (Lit. pig slop).

CHOCHEM: (CHOchem). A wise man; a know-it-all; a wise guy referred to with sarcasm. Yiddish is full of words with double meanings and CHOCHEM is one of them. COCHMEHS can be wisdom, a bright saying, a witticism most often said sarcastically. As typical of Jewish women, my mother would serve a full plate of food even if asked for a small portion. When Lester and I had company for dinner and dessert was to be served, I would ask if a large or small portion was wanted as some were fussy about calories. Before they could answer, Lester would say; "There are no COCHMEHS with Barbara. You will get what you ask for."

CHUTZPAH: (CHUTZpah). Unmitigated gall; brazenness, nerve, audacity, impudence. "A Jew is twenty-eight percent fear, two percent sugar, and seventy percent chutzpah." Yiddish proverb.

Peter Harris (see BLINTZ: A VERB) was the Chief of Staff for Senator Howard Metzenbaum for eight years. He said that was where he got the "extra CHUTZPAH" needed to ask people for donations for political purposes.

Knowing I was going to a Naples Community Concert which was celebrating the 100th birthday of Leonard Bernstein, I cogitated as to whether I had the nerve - CHUTZPAH - to try to get a copy of my book *Reminiscences and Recipes* to Maestro Rabinovitsj as it had a quip in it from Carl Little's book *Beverly Hallam: An Odyssey in Art* about Leonard Bernstein's father and Beverly Hallam's mother. Mr. Bernstein sold beauty supplies and Mrs. Hallam was a beautician. They talked about their children and Mr Bernstein said, "My Lennie wants to be a composer of music, a musician. I can't stand it. What is your daughter going to do?" "She is going to be an artist," said Mrs. Hallam with pride. Mr. Bernstein: "Oh my God. They're both going to starve to death." I asked a woman at the ticket desk if she thought Maestro would like the story. "Sure. I'll get it to Max." After the concert, I saw Maestro chatting with some concert goers and my usual reserve vanished as I introduced myself to him as the woman from Maine who wrote the book. "I met my wife in Maine. Mary, come over here and meet this woman from Maine." They were coming to Bar Harbor in August and I invited them to lunch. They came and we have been friends since.

Lester's Hydrangeas, Beverly Hallam

Barbara's Dessert, Beverly Hallam

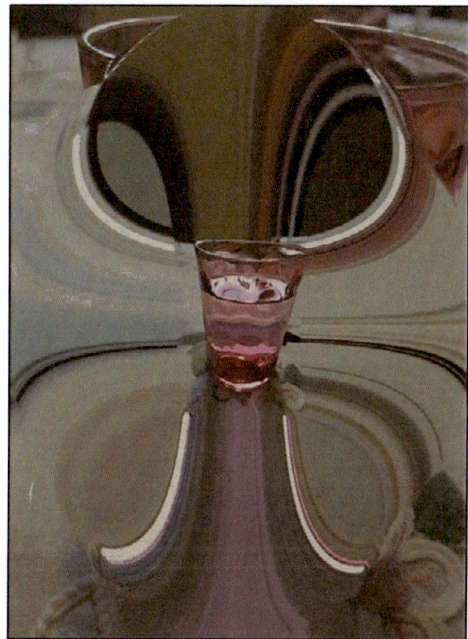

The Jolovitz Pink Glass, Beverly Hallam

COCKAMAMIE: (COCKaMAmie). Something ridiculous, incredible, crazy, foolish, non-sensible, et cetera. Although cockamamie does not have Yiddish lineage, it became a pet word of Jews and has become part of the Yiddish lexicon.

EYN SILABLE YIDDISH

In March 1911 newspaper editor Arthur Brisbane coined the adage "Use a picture. It's worth a thousand words." One word is a Yiddish picture. To wit:

ECH: A groan, a disparaging remark.
ECH MIR: A humorous disparaging remark.
EI: Oh! Oh dear!
ESS: Eat!
FEH: Fooey. It's no good.
FRESS: To eat a lot without restraint.
FRUM: Devout or pious.
GAI: Go. Leave.
KLOP: A hard punch.
KLOTZ: Ungraceful, awkward.
K'VELL: To glow with pride.
K'VETSH: To complain.
NAR: A fool.
NOSH: Nibble.
NOSHER: One who noshes between meals.
NU? So?
OY! Disgust, pain; astonishment.
SHA! Keep quiet.
TA'AM: Taste, flavor; good taste.
VEY: Woe, pain. Often said as OY VEY: dear me. OY VEY IZ MIR: woe is me.
ZETZ: A shove or push. A slap.

SARAH'S ZEYDE

Sarah Rockford belongs to the Yiddish class and is part of Bubbe's World. She is the Program Coordinator for "The Center for Small Town Jewish Life" at Colby College. She wanted to share her remembrance of her grandfather, her Zeyde.

"My maternal grandfather (Zeyde) spoke Yiddish as a first language. Sometimes he would walk around the house singing to himself in Yiddish, but I don't think I ever heard him speak it. He DID greet everyone by gregariously sweeping into a room asking "Hey, what's cooking?" It was such a signature phrase of his, and now I think that it must have been a translation from a colloquialism from his childhood in Poland. It's a very sweet remembrance of him for sure."

Post Script. September, 2021. Sarah has moved to New York to begin studies to become a rabbi.

TIFFANY'S IMAH'S SCHMATTA

My friend Tiffany wanted to share remembering her grandmother, Charlotte Kornhauser, who was called **IMAH** (Hebrew for grandmother) by her family:

"A fond memory I have of visiting my grandmother out on Long Island, N.Y. was how she dressed...

When we arrived from our home in the Catskills, she was always eagerly awaiting at the door, hair done, dressed nicely and adorned with fun jewelry. Her welcoming hug was the best, even though she was petite in stature, she grabbed you and didn't let go! Next was the welcome buffet of treats...always a delight and always too much before dinner. Food was her way to share her love to her family. But after the meal...just as her chicken soup with matzah balls comforted our souls, she would slip into her own source of comfort...her **SCHMATTA!**

The Yiddish word for rags, schmattas were comfy clothes and never worn out, just reserved for daily living. She would announce that it was schmatta time, and thus her work in entertaining and feeding us would conclude for the evening.

Were we to be busy preparing for larger holiday meals with as many as 20 people, she would wear her schmatta for the day as she boiled, baked and toiled over the huge meal, only to then change out of her schmatta, into her 'good' clothes, as the matriarch of our family."

A YIDDISH POEM

by Gene Wilder

Yiddish was the secret code, therefore I don't farshtaist,
A bisseleh maybe here and there, the rest has gone to waste.
Sadly when I hear it now, I only get the gist,
My Bubbe spoke it beautifully; but me, I am tsemisht.

So oy vey as I should say, or even oy vei iz mir,
Though my pisk is lacking Yiddish, it's familiar to my ear.
And I'm no Chaim Yonkel, in fact it was shtick naches,
But, when it comes to Yiddish though, I'm talking out my tuchas.

Es iz a shandeh far di kinder that I don't know it better
(Though it's really nishtgefelecht when one needs to write a letter).
But, when it comes to characters, there's really no contention,
No other linguist can compete with honorable mentshen:

They have nebbishes and rebechels and others without mazel,
Then, too, schmendriks and schlemiels, and let's not forget shlemazel.
These words are so precise and descriptive to the listener,
So much better than "a pill" is to call someone 'farbissener'.

Or - that a brazen woman would be better called Choleria,
And you'll agree farklempt says more than does hysteria.
I'm not haken dir a tshainik and I hope I'm not a kvetch,
But isn't mieskeit kinder, than to call someone a wretch?

Mitten derinnen, I hear Bubbe say, "It's nechtiker tog, don't fear,
To me you're still a maven, zol zein shah, don't fill my ear.
A leben ahf dein keppele, I don't mean to interrupt,
But you are speaking narishkeit…
And…A gezunt auf dein kop."

MENTSH: (MENTsh). A special human being.

MENTSH is a German word meaning "human being" and Yiddish took it a step further. Calling someone a mentsh is the highest compliment you can give someone. A mentsh is a person who acts with honor, humility, integrity, is kind and considerate.

Grandsons Ben, Will, Nicky, and Madison, a grandson by association, on the 50th anniversary of the founding of YMCA Camp Tracy, announced the formation of the Camp Tracy Alumni Association in recognition of its three founders, George Keller, Richard Hawkes, and their grandfather Lester Jolovitz. Zayde told the boys his father instilled in him the importance of being a mentsh and he expected no less from his grandsons. Acting with honor, humility, integrity, kindness and consideration, these young men established the Renaissance Scholarship which provides financial assistance for children to attend Camp Tracy. It is the goal of the Alumni Association to be sure Camp Tracy will continue in the future to be a safe place for children as envisioned by the three founders. Zayde's admonition to his grandsons did not go unheeded. They are the mentshen he wanted them to be.

Back l-r: Ben, Will, Madison, & Nicky. Front: Ken Walsh, CEO Alfond Youth Center.

The Jolovitz Outdoor Theatre in the background.

Camp Tracy founders George Keller, Richard Hawkes, and Lester Jolovitz

RACHMONES (RachMONes) literally means compassion and includes mercy, empathy and forgiveness. It is derived from the Hebrew root word **RECHEM** meaning womb. Leo Rosten in *The Joys of Yiddish* explains the concept that "one should look upon others with the same love and feeling that a mother feels for the issue in her womb."

Anne Frank wrote in her autobiography:

"In spite of everything, I still believe that people are really good at heart. I simply can't build up my hopes on a foundation consisting of confusion, misery and death. I see the world gradually being turned into a wilderness, I hear that ever-approaching thunder, which will destroy us, too. I can feel the sufferings of millions and yet, if I look up into the heavens, I think that it will all come right, that this cruelty too will end."

"I can feel the sufferings of millions..." Rachmones.

KLEZMER

The best-known Jewish music form is KLEZMER (KLEZmer). The word combines the Yiddish words klei (instrument) and zemer (song). Klezmer emerged in The Middle Ages in the Jewish ghettos and shtetls of Eastern Europe. The music was based on the instruments available — fiddles, guitars, pianos, cellos, cymbals, drums, clarinets, accordions, brass instruments — and became an important part of entertainment. It was listened to, danced to, featured the virtuosity of some of the players and eventually became associated with weddings and bar mitzvahs. It came to America with the immigrants and continued to be played at weddings, bar/bat mitzvahs, other celebrations and

Yiddish theater. Perhaps the most recognized Klezmer sound is the opening clarinet glissando in George Gershwin's "Rhapsody in Blue."

"Violins of Hope" is a collection of mostly Klezmer stringed instruments played by European Jews in the ghettos and then in concentration camps. Several years ago, those instruments started appearing in Israel for repair by renowned violin maker Amnon Weinstein who researched their histories and wanted to share them and the instruments with the world. In 2020 four of those instruments made their way to the Naples, Florida Holocaust Museum where they were lovingly played in a string quartet led by Maestro Max Rabinovitsj, a Holocaust survivor.

"Where there were violins, there was hope." Amnon Weinstein.

Maestro Max Rabinovitsj

MY NEIGHBOR

Brian Bray became my neighbor a few years ago when he and his two Bichon Frisé dogs moved into the house across the street. They moved in during the winter, were waiting for my return from Florida to meet me, and much to Brian's pleasure, got welcomed with cookies. Brian gets a daily dose of Yiddish and he will occasionally email me "I know that word." It did not take long for him to be part of Bubbe's World. Brian has shared his work with Holocaust Museum in St. Louis:

"I worked at the St. Louis Holocaust Museum and Learning Center from 1998 - 2003 as Director of Administration and Development. Prior to my working there, I periodically heard Yiddish phrases (schlep, meshuggeneh, kvetch, oy vey, etc.) but never gave much thought about the language. However, I became more immersed in the language while working at the museum and while getting to know the many Holocaust survivors who volunteered at the museum (at one time, there were more than 300 survivors living in St. Louis).

One of the projects that I managed at the museum was to digitize the oral history project - the museum began recording testimonies of Holocaust survivors in the 1970s but the videos and tapes sat on the dusty shelves in the storage area of the museum. I helped transcribe the testimonies and hired a media company to transfer them to a digital format so that the recordings would be preserved. It was through these stories that I developed an appreciation for the Yiddish language as well as a love for the survivors.

The survivors, docents and volunteers embraced and welcomed me at the museum and I developed many lifelong friendships through my work at the museum. They affectionately referred to me as a mensch, which filled my heart with joy.

My work at the museum was the richest and most rewarding professional experience I've ever had and I still have many fond memories of my time there."

BEI MIR BISTU SHEYN

"BEI MIR BISTU SHEYN" "By Me You Are Beautiful" is perhaps the most famous song from Yiddish theater. It came from the musical comedy "I Would If I Could" which in Yiddish was "Men Ken Lebn Lost Nisht" – "You could live, but they won't let you." The play was performed in 1932 and closed after one season. The fame of the song came from a recording by the Andrews Sisters in 1937. The title "BEI MIR BISTU SHEYN" was given a Germanic spelling: "Bei Mir Bist Du Schön."

"BEI MIR BISTU SHEYN"

Vay bei mir bistu sheyn,
bei mir hostu kheyn,
bei mir, bistu eyner af der velt.

Because to me you're beautiful,
to me you have grace,
to me, you're one of a kind.

Bei mir bistu gut,
bei mir hostu "it,"
bei mir bistu tayerer fun gelt.
Felt sheyne meydlekh hobn shon gevolt nemen mikh
un fun zey ale oysgeklibn hob ikh nor dikh.
Vayl bei mir bistu sheyn,
bei mir hostu kheyn
bei mir, bistu eyner af der velt.

To me, you're great,
to me you have "it,"
to me you're more precious than riches.
Many beautiful girls have wanted me
and from all of them I chose only you.
Because to me you're beautiful,
to me you have grace,
to me, you're one of a kind.

The Andrews Sisters

HAYLEY'S MAISEH

Hayley Deeter has an art gallery and design business in New Albany, Ohio. As one who gets a daily dose of Yiddish and is part of Bubbe's World, Hayley wanted to share her Yiddish **MAISEH** (story):

"My mother used to always say Drahd (sp?) as in hub-say teef tyre en drahd which meant as 'go to hell' but the Yiddish literal I believe means 'make like an onion with your head in the dirt.'

Drahd was her go-to word for anytime she had something bad to say. She also said something like 'gay cockem afam yon' and I only know gay means go. She also said alta cocka a lot to refer to an old person.

She also used shvatza a lot which is a no-no, faygala, also a no-no and anyone was a goy who wasn't Jewish. She was not a very empathetic, enlightened, or patient person. People she didn't like were schmucks, schmendricks, chazzahs, and meiskite if they were ugly. She said feh a lot and I use that word often. Food she didn't like was chazahry and anyone overly made up was ungapatchked - does this make sense to you?

She characterized people often and separated them into categories which I would never do. But that was her way - she was born in 1917 in a foreign country and that's how she was taught. It was an us against them type of upbringing since her father was killed by the Bolsheviks during the revolution before they made the long and arduous trip from Russia to LeHavre, France, and then to Ellis Island and finally to Borough Park Brooklyn.

Does this give you perspective?

Thanks for allowing me to share with you."

Hayley's Gallery

"THE HEBREW RACE HAS BEEN WAITING 4000 YEARS FOR CRISCO"

That is how in 1910 Procter and Gamble advertised the invention of a totally vegetable shortening, claiming it was "cheap and kosher." In 1933, Procter and Gamble published a bilingual booklet *Crisco Recipes for the Jewish Housewife* in Yiddish and English with about sixty recipes. Its advertisements in the Yiddish press showed Brooklyn and Bronx housewives making potato pancakes and strudel with Crisco.

KASHRUTH: (KASHruth) is a set of dietary laws dealing with the foods Jews are permitted to eat. Food that may be eaten is deemed KOSHER which is Yiddish for the Hebrew term kashér meaning "fit" (for consumption).

"Do not cook a young goat in its mother's milk." Deuteronomy 14:21. The idea was that milk and meat should not be eaten at the same time. Details and how they were to be applied were set down later in oral laws and elaborated in further rabbinical literature, suggesting they were a test for obedience, philosophical, practical and hygienic reasons.

FLEISHIG: (FLEIshig). Foods that contain meat.
MILCHIG: (MILchig). Foods that contain dairy.
PAREVE: (PAREVE). Food that is neither meat nor dairy.
TRAIF: (TRAIF) Not kosher; not edible.
ESS GEZUNTERHAIT! (ESS GeZUNterHAIT!) Eat in good health!

CHALLAH: (CHAllah) is an ancient Hebrew word meaning a kind of loaf or cake and became part of the Yiddish lexicon as a braided bread for Shabbat, Friday night dinner. After candles are lit and blessed, wine is poured, blessed and drunk, the CHALLAH is uncovered, blessed and a piece is sliced and torn to share with those present. It is usually made with oil and water which keeps it PAREVE to enjoy with meat or dairy.

My daughter Debbie's Rosh Hashanah challah is symbolically round
for the start of the Jewish New Year.

Charles Louis Fleischmann did not like the taste of American bread. Before immigrating to America, he was in the distilling and yeast business in Hungary. He went back to Hungary and returned to America with his baker brother, a variety of yeasts and went into the yeast business. When my mother needed yeast, she would send me to a nearby bakery for "three cents yeast." In the late nineteenth century, people became so accustomed to buying their yeast that the amount listed in cookbooks was "one or two cents yeast." Fleischmann began packaging fresh yeast cakes for sale in grocery stores and dried yeast became available after World War ll.

Debbie's Recipe
Makes 2 large loaves:

In mixer bowl, combine and let set 5 minutes:
2 yeast
1/4 c. warm water
1 tsp. sugar
After 5 minutes, add and combine: 1 3/4 c. warm water
1/4 c. sugar 1/4 c. honey.

Add:
3 eggs, beaten, 1/2 c. Canola oil, 2 1/2 tsp. salt
7- 8 c. unbleached flour

Egg wash
(Sesame or poppy seeds)

Combine and knead for 5 minutes. Oil a bowl; place dough in bowl, cover, let rise until doubled (1 - 1 1/2 hours).

Gently deflate the dough and remove from the bowl to be shaped. Cut dough in half and each half in thirds. Form dough into 3 lengths, braid and place on a baking sheet lined with parchment paper; cover and let rise 30 minutes. Brush with egg wash and sprinkle with seeds, if desired. Bake 25 minutes. 350° oven.

BABKA: (BABka) is the quintessential Jewish pastry. Declaring a woman a **BALEBOSTEH** (BALeBOSteh), a good homemaker, often depended on her babka. The dough is made and rises overnight in the refrigerator. It is then rolled out, spread with butter, sprinkled with cinnamon and brown sugar, raisins and chopped nuts, rolled up and placed in bread pans, strewn with crumbs and set aside to rise; when doubled in size, it is baked. Chocolate-filled babka appeared in New York bakeries in the late 1950s.

Mrs. Jolovitz was known for her babka which she would make for family get-to-gethers on Saturday nights in their apartment above the grocery store. Rosh Hashanah is my annual babka baking. The first time I made it for Lester, I knew I was delving into the memory of his mother's babka. He declared mine had the right **TA'AM** (taste). It was toasted for breakfast the next day: "My mother would never let my father eat it for breakfast. Babka was for company."

My babka recipe with a traditional filling follows. Grandson Ben adapted his chocolate-filled babka recipe from *Cook's Illustrated* cookbook.

BARBARA'S BABKA

1/2 lb. butter, softened
1/2 c. sugar
3 eggs
1/2 c. sour cream
3 yeast
1 tsp. salt
5/6 c. unbleached flour
1 c. milk.

Filling: Softened butter, brown sugar, cinnamon, chopped walnuts, golden raisins

Crumb topping: 1/4 c. butter, 1/2 c. flour, 1/2 c. sugar, cinnamon

Egg Wash: 1 egg beaten with 1 T. of water.

In the bowl of a mixer, cream butter and sugar. Add eggs, sour cream and yeast. Beat well. Add salt to flour and alternate with milk to the batter. Mix thoroughly until a soft but firm ball is formed. Cover and let rise in the same bowl overnight in the refrigerator. Let stand at room temperature for 15 minutes before rolling out.

Divide dough in thirds. Roll out to a rectangle, spread with butter, strew with brown sugar, raisins and chopped walnuts; roll up from the narrow side and place in parchment paper lined loaf pans.

Combine the crumb topping with the dough on the sides of the bowl. Brush babka with egg wash, sprinkle with crumbs, cover, and let rise until doubled.

Bake in a 350° oven until browned, approximately 40 - 45 minutes. Place on a wire rack to cool for 15 minutes; then remove from pans to cool completely.

BEN'S BABKA

4 c. unbleached flour

3 tsp. instant yeast
1 tsp salt
1 c. milk, room temperature
1/2 c. sugar
4 eggs, separated, reserving 2 whites for filling
2 tsp. vanilla
1/2 pound unsalted butter, softened.

Filling:
4 oz. semi-sweet or bittersweet chocolate, chopped
8 T. unsalted butter
6 T. cocoa
1/2 c. confectioners sugar
2 egg whites

Egg Wash: 1 egg beaten with 1 T. water.

Whisk together milk, sugar, egg yolks and vanilla. In the mixing bowl, whisk together flour, yeast and salt. Using dough hook and low speed, gradually drizzle milk mixture into the flour until dough starts to come together.

At medium speed and using the dough hook, add the butter, 1 tablespoon at a time, until it is incorporated into the dough.

Continue kneading about 10 minutes until the dough is smooth and elastic. Remove the dough to a floured board and shape into a smooth ball which is placed in a greased bowl, cover tightly with plastic wrap; let rise until increased by half. Place in refrigerator for about an hour until dough is firm or overnight. Let stand at room temperature about 15 minutes before rolling out.

Prepare the filling, combining the chocolate, butter, and cocoa in a bowl and place in the microwave at medium power for 1 minute. Stir. Repeat for 15 or 30 seconds until the chocolate mixture is melted and smooth. Add the confectioner's sugar and blend until smooth. Cool; beat egg whites with a fork until smooth and add to chocolate mixture. Reserve 2 T. of mixture.

Ben's Babka

350° oven. Line two 8 1/2 inch x 4 1/2 inch bread pans with parchment paper. Spray with Pam.

Gently deflate the dough and place on a floured surface. Divide dough in half. Press or roll the dough to an 18 x 14-inch rectangle. Spread the filling over the dough leaving a half-inch border. Roll up with the longer side facing you and pinch ends together. Reshape if needed to keep the 18 inches. With seam side up, spread half of the reserved chocolate along the seam. Fold the dough in half bringing it on top of itself. Pinch the ends together to seal.

Gently twist the dough twice to form a double figure eight. Lift the dough into the prepared pan, pressing the dough into the corners of the pan. Lightly cover and let dough rise to the edge of the pan. Brush with the egg wash and bake on lower middle oven rack for 40 - 45 minutes or until it is a deep golden brown. Cool in the pan for 15 minutes and remove to a wire rack.

BEYGL vs. BIALY

BEYGL, its Yiddish spelling, have become available everywhere. They are round like a donut and that is where the similarity ends. BEYGL, now known as BAGEL, are made from a yeast dough, boiled and baked. Before baking, they can be covered with sesame seeds or poppy seeds, onions, salt, "everything" or plain. The boiling and baking helps keep the bagel fresh longer and the hole provides an even bake. The hole also served as a place to stack the bagel on a stick when they were sold on the streets of the Lower East Side.

Originating in Poland, the first known mention of "bajgiel" was in Poland in 1610 in the Jewish community of Kraków and were eaten by Ashkenazi Jews from the 17th Century on. Beygl is from the German word "bougel" meaning ring or bracelet. Once split in half, it is topped with a **SCHMEAR** (cream cheese), **LOX** (smoked salmon), a slice of red onion, tomato, capers, or just spread with butter or peanut butter. Bagel have become an integral part of Sunday breakfast, and are included in brunch buffets everywhere.

BIALY is a Yiddish word short for "Bialystoker Kuchen" which originated in the Polish city of Bialystok in the 19th Century. Jews ate so many of them that non-Jews started calling the Jews "Bialystoker kuchen fressers" - bialy eaters. It is a small chewy roll round like a bagel but is not boiled and has no hole in the middle. It has a depression in the middle which is filled with diced onions and poppy seeds. Brought to America in the late 1800s by Polish refugees, bialys were baked mostly in Brooklyn, and became as much a part of Sunday breakfast as bagel. Though usually torn apart and spread with butter or cream cheese, they are also sliced, lightly toasted and spread with butter or cream cheese. They are also eaten with the usual bagel accompaniments.

Mister Bagel, a "New York bagel" shop, opened in Portland in 1977. Its owner was from Brooklyn and brought the first good bagel to Maine. Bialys were also part of the business but were made from bagel dough with an indentation for the onion and poppy seeds. Having had Brooklyn bialys and it was obvious to me they were bagel made to look like bialy, I said to the owner, "Those aren't bialys!" Rick: "Shhh. No one around here knows that."

KICHEL

KICHEL (KIChel), originating in Eastern Europe, is a light, airy and crunchy cookie rolled out flat and cut into bow tie shapes and twisted in the middle. They are a popular sweet snack in Israel, and Jews in South Africa eat them with chopped herring. My mother's kichel, though crunchy, were not light and airy. My daughter Debbie's kichel, on the other hand, are light, airy and have a crunchy breath of sweetness.

DEBBIE'S KICHEL

6 eggs
1/2 tsp. vanilla
3/4 c. Canola oil
2-1/3 c. unbleached flour
1 tsp. salt
1 c. sugar

375° oven.

Place ingredients in bowl of mixer and blend on low speed. When combined, beat on high speed for 5 minutes. Rest the dough, covered, for an hour.

Sprinkle the sugar onto the work surface about 1/8 inch deep. Remove the dough from the bowl (it will be sticky) and shape into a ball. Place the ball of dough in the center of the work surface, flatten slightly and sprinkle liberally with sugar.

Roll the dough into a rectangle about 18 x 24 inches. Cut the dough into strips 3/4 inch wide and 2 inches long. Twist each strip in the middle to make into a bow tie and place on cookie sheets lined with parchment paper, leaving a little space between each.

Bake the kichlech 25 - 30 minutes, switching cookie sheets midway. They will be hard on all corners and light brown. Test for doneness by breaking one in half; if it is doughy or soft, bake a few minutes longer.

RUGELACH

RUGELACH is a Yiddish word meaning "little twists" and considered a cookie. Originating in Poland and called "rogale," they were introduced in this country by immigrants from Poland, Germany, and other Eastern European countries. The dough was made with sour cream and yeast and filled with fruits, jams, nuts, and spices. When rugelach got to this country, they were made with a cream cheese dough and a bit of sour cream. The dough is rolled into circles, spread with jam, sprinkled with sugar and cinnamon, chopped nuts and raisins, and then cut into triangles and rolled up like crescents. It can also be rolled out into a rectangle, covered with filling, rolled up and cut into circles. Following is my recipe for rugelach made with sour cream, rolled into a rectangle and sliced into circles.

PASTRY:
2 c. unbleached flour
Pinch salt
2 sticks cold butter
3/4 c. sour cream
1 egg yolk

FILLING:

Apricot preserves
Raspberry jam
Cinnamon and sugar
Finely chopped walnuts
Currants or raisins

Barbara's Rugelach

375° oven, parchment paper lined cookie sheets. Makes about 4 dozen.

Combine flour and salt in a bowl. Cut in butter and combine with flour until butter is the size of peas. Mix egg yolk into sour cream and stir into flour mixture until well combined. Remove dough to plastic wrap and refrigerate until well chilled or overnight.

Divide dough into four pieces. Roll into rectangles about 12 inches long and spread two with apricot preserves and two with raspberry jam. Sprinkle with cinnamon and sugar, nuts, and currants. Roll up and cut into one-inch circles. Place on a cookie sheet lined with parchment paper and sprinkle with cinnamon and sugar. Bake about 20 minutes or until browned.

Remove from oven to wire rack to cool. When cool, place in a container with waxed paper between layers. Refrigerate. Can be frozen.

SCHÜTTEHEREIN

SCHÜTTEHEREIN (SCHÜTteheREIN). To cook without a recipe by adding a little of this, a little of that and taste it until it had the right taste. That was how my mother cooked and I learned watching her as she would "schütteherein." Recipes for pastries were more exact, calling for two glasses of flour, a little less than a glass of sugar, a pinch of salt, et cetera. In 1901, *The Settlement Cookbook* was published by Lizzie Black Kander, a social worker in Milwaukie, Wisconsin, as a cookbook for mostly Russian immigrants. The recipes were not all Jewish foods but those that were came with Mrs. Kanter's Eastern European family.

A Holocaust cookbook, *In Memories Kitchen: A Legacy from the Women of Terezin* was Mrs. Mina Paechter's "kochbuch" compiled with sixty-five recipes combined from starving Jewish Czechoslovakian women in the concentration camp Terezin. Their recipes included "Gesundheitkuchen," the good health cake brought to the mothers of newborn babies, "Linzertortes" served at tea parties and Czech Jewish "Mazelkich," a layered matzo and fruit dessert for Passover. It was their common hope that by putting together a "kochbuch," the shards of paper with their recipes would serve as their memories, that their dreams and legacies would live on. This is the book's foreword:

"Their thoughts were inevitably and ceasely focused on food. Discussion of its preparation and the heated arguments concerning the superiority of one method over another served as more than an anodyne for their tortured nerves. It strengthened their resolve to survive if only because it made more vivid, not what they sought to escape from, but what they were resolved to return to."

Their legacy, like the violins of Auschwitz, survived but the women, like the violinists, did not.

Following are a few known Jewish foods. Their names are Yiddish as they came with the immigrants from mostly Eastern Europe:

BORSHT: Beet soup.

CHOLENT. TSHOLNT: Hearty stew.

GEDEMPTE FLEISH: Potted meat.

GEFILTE FISH: Poached fish balls.

GEHAKTEH LEBER: Chopped liver.

HOLISHKES: Stuffed cabbage.

HUMMUS: Puréed chickpeas.

KNAIDLACH: Matzo balls.

KUGEL: A sweet or savory casserole made with noodles (lokshen).

LATKES: Potato pancakes.

MATZO BREI: An omelet made with pieces of water-softened matzo added to the eggs.

TSIMMIS: A sweet carrot dish.

CHOLENT. TSHOLNT.

CHOLENT is Anglicized from the Polish word TSHOLNT. This hearty stew was first mentioned in the 1180 writing of Rabbi Yitzhak in Vienna. The ingredients then, as now, were put into a pot, covered and baked 12 or more hours. Conforming to Jewish laws that cooking was prohibited on the Sabbath, the stew was put together on Friday, put into a slow oven before sunset and ready for Saturday lunch. Before ovens were in the home, the pot was taken to the shtetl baker for overnight cooking as the

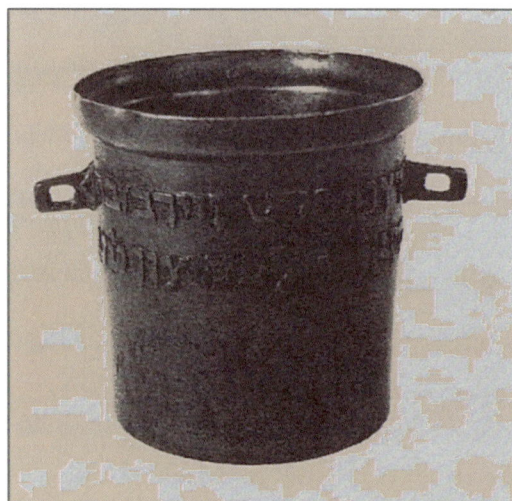

Cholent Pot

bakery oven was always fired up. The ingredients varied using beef and/or chicken, potatoes, beans and barley. Onions, garlic and spices were added, depending on the cook. Sometimes molasses was added for a touch of sweet and color. Cholent is now cooked in slow cookers.

Cholent was eaten everywhere and made with similar basic ingredients which included locally available meats such as turkey, chicken, goose and vegetables such as carrots, sweet potatoes and eggplant. The name was different, but you were eating cholent everywhere: Poland: czulent; Germany, The Netherlands, and European countries: schalet, shalent or shalet; Hungary: sólet; Morocco: s'hina or skhina; Spain: adafina or dafina; Iraq: t'bit'; Ethiopia: doro wat.

(Post Script. October 13, 2021. The television program "Jeopardy!" had a SABBATH category. One of the questions was "What is Cholent?" The contestants did not know Cholent was "a Jewish stew traditionally eaten on the Sabbath."

GEFILTE FISH

GEFILTE (GeFILte) FISH is Yiddish for "stuffed fish." Originally, the fish mixture was stuffed into the skin of a whole fish. It is made from freshwater fish such as carp, whitefish, pike and buffalo ground with onions and added eggs, matzo meal, salt and pepper. Hands are wet and ready for a scoop of the fish mixture to be shaped in balls and gently dropped into simmering stock made with sliced carrots and onions (including the outer peel for color) and fish bones. My mother would slice up some of the skin into 1/2-inch-wide strips, place a strip into her wet palm, place a scoop of fish on it and wrap the rest of the skin around the fish. Not all were wrapped in skin. She also stuffed the head of the fish for my father. Gefilte fish is eaten year 'round but is the traditional first course at the Passover Seder. The fish is decorated with a slice of carrot from the stock in which the fish cooked and a sprinkle of parsley. I do not make gefilte fish.

Gefilte fish always brings to mind the sad story of my mother putting her pot of gefilte fish on the back porch to keep chilled overnight. Those were the days when garbage was picked up from the back porch. The garbage man didn't know from gefilte fish.

GEHAKTEH LEBER (GeHAKteh LEber). Chopped liver.

Literally. GEHAKTEH LEBER is made with chicken livers fried with onions, hard boiled eggs, **SHMALTZ** (rendered chicken fat), salt and pepper. The ingredients are combined in a processor, but they can be mashed together which gives more texture. Once combined, additional shmaltz, salt and pepper is added to taste. It is eaten with crackers, matzo or celery. My mother used to "decorate" her gehakteh leber with sieved hard-boiled egg yolk.

Shmaltz is made by frying chicken fat and skins and chopped onion. The rendered pieces are **GRIBBENES** (GRIBbenES) which are crunchy and delicious. Gribbenes and crackling are the same thing, albeit from different animals.

Figuratively. Used in the sense that if someone felt excluded or unworthy, they would say: "What am I - chopped liver?"

TSIMMES

TSIMMES (TSIMmes) is an Ashkenazi Jewish sweetened stew, made with carrots like my mother's, or a combination of vegetables, such as carrots, potatoes and sweet potatoes, and dried fruits such as prunes and apricots, and honey. A piece of meat is usually included for flavor and a bit of fat. TSIMMES comes from the Yiddish words tzim (for) and esn (eating). It is traditionally served at Rosh Hashanah to start the New Year with something sweet. You can also make a tsimmes about something which is a big fuss or much ado about nothing.

PETER'S GRANNY'S TSIMMIS

Peter Harris was mentioned in BLINTZES. We talked about tsimmes one day and his granny's was not like my mother's. I asked him if he would share her recipe.

GRANNY'S TSIMMIS:

"My granny came over from what she used to call White Russia. She never told me the name of the village. She worked selling from a pushcart as a child and sent money back to bring family members and villagers over. They started businesses too and when I would visit her as a child and we went shopping on West 72nd street the bakery and other shopkeepers would always put something (actually quite a bit) extra in her bag for free, because 'Aunt Minnie' had helped get their family to America.

Granny never wrote her recipes down, and often told me about their components in qualitative terms, like 'the water should be salty like Coney Island not Miami Beach' or 'moist like the white fish we get at Gellises'.

She always made a lot of food; I know she was often hungry as a child. When we ate at other people's houses the biggest sin of another cook was stinginess of portions, like 'When there are eight guests she only cooks seven ears of corn.' Said with sad disapproval!

She kept kosher and cooked everything in a way that the phrase 'mouth-watering' was a perfect descriptor. One of my favorites was her tsimmis. I can only describe it by saying it was a composed dish because of how the ingredients were arranged in rows in the pan for roasting.

Take an oblong roasting pan. Make rows of, in this order, short ribs with enough fat, sweet potatoes, prunes, carrots, prunes (sometimes dried apricots too), sweet potatoes and finish up with short ribs. Repeat as dictated by number of servings needed and size of pan.

Pour in some homemade beef broth with plenty, but not too much, honey. Salt a little less than Coney Island.

Place on top potato balls which I think were really her latke recipe shaped into balls of a size between ping pong balls and golf balls.

Roast it at about 350° in a small apartment oven (wonderful what she could do in that tiny apartment at 70th and West End) covered for a while, then uncovered and frequently basted with the honeyed juices so nothing dried out and the prunes stayed plump and be sure to get a deep golden crust on the potato balls, the sweet potatoes and the carrots.

No measurements, she was an artist."

MY MOTHER'S TSIMMES

My mother's TSIMMES was unlike any other. It was a casserole made with carrots, an onion, a piece of fatty meat and a potato **KUGEL** (pudding) covering it. The kugel is what made it unique. A tsimmes was made at Passover so the kugel had to be made with matzo meal. It is the same batter as used for **LATKES** (potato pancakes), except they are made with flour. Potatoes were grated on a "ribizen" which in today's culinary terms is a "four-sided grater." We all grated which included a bit of knuckle. Now, potatoes are shredded in a processor. I use a blender.

KUGEL is known more as a baked casserole made from **LOKSHEN** (egg noodles), cottage cheese, cream cheese, sour cream, (raisins), eggs and a little sugar. It can also be made with apples and no dairy which makes it pareve. The word KUGEL came from Middle High German which meant sphere, globe ball. The Yiddish name originated from the German description as the kugel was originally baked in round dishes.

In a large roasting pan, place 3 lb. of baby carrots, about 1 1/2 pounds of meat, 1 whole onion, honey, salt and pepper. Cover with cold water and bake in a 325° oven. Meanwhile, make the potato kugel:

2 eggs
8 large russet potatoes, peeled and chunked
1 large onion, peeled and chunked
Matzo meal
Salt and Pepper.

Crack 1 egg into the blender and add a few pieces of potato and onion. Pulse until combined. Continue adding potato and onion until the blender jar is 3/4 full. Pour mixture into a bowl and repeat. 325° oven, 4 - 5 hours.

Spoon off some of the water that has collected around the edge of the kugel mixture. Stir in about 1/2 - 3/4 c. matzo meal, salt and pepper. Taste to be sure it has enough seasoning. Pour over the carrots and meat and continue cooking four to five hours. If the kugel starts getting too brown, lay a piece of foil over the top. Add water around the edges so the mixture does not dry out.

If serving the tsimmes the same day as made, uncover and let it brown and become crisp. If serving the next day, cool, cover and refrigerate. Allow to come to room temperature before reheating. Heat at 350° for a couple of hours, with the foil loose on top, checking to make sure it is not drying out. Add water around the edges if needed. Uncover the last half hour or so until the kugel has crisped up.

FRUIT TSIMMES

Fruit Tsimmes is also known as COMPOTE, a dish made with fresh or dried fruits that have been slowly cooked in a sugar syrup with preferred spices such as cinnamon, allspice, and whole cloves. It is served warm or chilled.

The word COMPOTE was derived from the Latin word "compositus" meaning mixture and originated in medieval Europe. It was believed that fruit cooked in a sugar syrup balanced the effects of humidity on the body. During the Renaissance, it was served chilled at the end of a meal. Being easy to prepare from inexpensive ingredients and containing no milk (pareve), compote was eaten by Jews throughout Europe and continues to be eaten year round but especially at Passover and Rosh Hashanah. Any or all of the following fruits are used in compote:

Dried apricots, pears, apples, cherries
Prunes
Golden raisins
A strip of lemon or orange rind
Cinnamon
Honey to taste
Water

Place fruits and spices in a pot. Cover with water. Bring to a boil, uncovered, reduce heat, simmer around 10 minutes; fruits should be a bit firm. They will absorb the syrup as they cool. Serve hot or chilled.

BABUSHKA'S KOMPOT

Granddaughter Amy grew up drinking BABUSHKA'S KOMPOT. Amy's Russian Babushka (grandmother) made Kompot from a combination of dried fruits which flavored the liquid they were cooked in and the liquid would be drunk warm or chilled.

Some people did not eat the fruit and strained it out but Amy's family would eat the fruit as they drank a Kompot. Amy calls it a Russian version of a fruit punch which tastes similar to Sangria.

About 12 cups water
30 ounces of any dried or fresh fruits (prunes, apples, apricots, cranberries, cherry, pear, etc.) Sugar, if desired.

Wash dry fruits, then soak in warm water for 15 minutes, wash again. Put fruit in the pot with water and bring to boil, add sugar and boil for 15 minutes. Let it cool. It is best to cook it in the evening to be served the next day. Can be served hot or cold. Fruit can be drained or eaten.

KNAIDLACH

SINGULAR: KNAIDL, KNAIDEL, KNEIDL, KNEIDEL.
PLURAL: KNAIDELS, KNAIDLACH, KNAIDELAH, KNEIDELS, KNEIDLACH, KNEIDELACH, KNEHDLS, KNEYDEL. KNEYDLACH.

Singular or plural, KNAIDEL and KNAIDLACH are MATZO BALLS.

They are an Ashkenzai Jewish soup dumpling, coming from the German word "knödel" or dumpling. German, Austrian and Alsation Jews were the first to prepare matzo balls for their soup.

In 1902, Sarah Tyson Rorer who wrote *Settlement Cookbook* published *Mrs. Rorer's Cookbook: A Manual for Housekeeping.* Included in the book were menus and a recipe for "Matzoth Balls." That is the first time knaidlach were referred to as matzo ball.

3 eggs, lightly beaten
1/4 c. Canola oil
1 medium size onion, chopped
1/4 - 1/2 c. water

1 bouillon cube
1 c. matzo meal
Salt
Pepper

Sauté onion in oil until translucent. Cool slightly and add to eggs with bouillon dissolved in the water, salt and a little pepper. Add enough matzo meal to make a stiff batter. Finger taste batter to make sure there is enough seasoning. Cover and set aside for at least half an hour.

Bring a large pot of salted water to a boil. Wet hands and form golf ball-size balls. Drop into boiling water. Lower heat to simmer. Cover and let cook for at least half an hour WITHOUT looking. Serve in soup sprinkled with chopped parsley.

Leftover matzo balls can be sprinkled with cinnamon and sugar, baked and served with chicken or meat.

"BEHOLD THE OLDEST KNOWN YIDDISH WRITING IN THE WORLD."

The following is from *The Forward* dated September 6, 2018:

A medieval Jewish manuscript bearing the oldest known example of the Yiddish language is making a rare public appearance at Israel's National Library in Jerusalem ahead of the High Holidays.

The Worms Mahzor, named for the German city where it was housed for centuries, is a richly illuminated codex from the 13th century containing the prayers for the holidays and other liturgical hymns for the congregation's cantor. The prayer book, with its medieval European cityscapes, bird-headed humans and menagerie of beasts was used by the Worms Jewish community for centuries, up until the rise of Nazi Germany in the 20th Century.

But hidden within the Hebrew prayers - written in red ink inside blank spaces within larger black letters of the first word of the Prayer for Dew for Passover - appears a wish of good tidings intended for the poor schlimazel tasked with schlepping the weighty tome to the synagogue.

"Gut tag im betage se vaer dis mahson in beith hakenseth trage." The Yiddish words read: "Let a good day shine for him, who will carry this mahzor to the synagogue."

"This is the first known example of written Yiddish in history," said Yoel Finkelman, curator of the National Library's Haim and Hanna Solomon Judaica Collection. An inscription inside the parchment codex informs us that it was completed on 28 Tevet 5032, or 2 January 1272, in the German city of Wörzburg by one "Simcha ben Yehudah, for his uncle, Rabbi Baruch ben Yitzhak," and that it took Simcha the scribe 4 weeks to complete the original two-volume set.

Finkelman said the Yiddish inscription is not only an important glimpse of the language in its early form but also suggested to historians that "beautiful mahzorim were owned by individuals and used by communities, unlike today where the synagogue owns the siddurim." A family might own a prayer book, but a tome of this size cost a flock of sheep and a year's worth of scribal work and decoration, making it more than most people could afford. Scholars believe that the Yiddish language emerged from German-speaking Jews living in cities along the Rhine around 1000 years ago. Worms, along with Cologne, Mainz, Speyer and Metz, were some of the prominent centers of Jewish life in the Rhineland where the language developed.

The Worms Mahzor plays an important role in discerning the nature of Yiddish in these developmental years, "From the linguistic point of view, it shows from the beginning Yiddish was what we call a fusion language, that on a Germanic basis it introduced words from Hebrew," said Professor Avraham Novershtern, head of the Yiddish studies department of the Hebrew University of Jerusalem.

The Yiddish inscription is largely German words and grammar, but two words - for mahzor and synagogue - are Hebrew, and the entirety of the inscription is in Hebrew script.

That blending of medieval German words and grammar with Hebrew, Aramaic and Slavic terminology produced a new tongue, which "signaled the beginning of a fundamentally new chapter in Jewish history - the Yiddish era," wrote the late historian Max Weinreich in his *History of the Yiddish Language*, which was finally published in its complete edition in 2008. Over the course of the centuries, Yiddish blossomed into the lingua franca of Ashkenazi Jews across the continent; by the 20th century, the globe.

But understanding the nature of the Yiddish language when the Worms Mahzor was written is no simple task. "We don't have many clues about the spoken language of the Jews at that time," Novershtern said. "Even if the language was not so different from the language of the surrounding population, their reading habits were radically different from them." The Yiddish text was written in Hebrew characters, and he said it's possible Ashkenazi Jews were not even literate in the Latin alphabet.

These early glimpses at the Yiddish language in its infancy are also extremely rare. "You have to realize that after this inscription from 1272, we have to make a leap of 110 years till the next dated document in Yiddish, that is in 1382," Novershtern said, referring to the Cambridge Codex, a Yiddish text found in the Cairo Geniza.

When exactly Yiddish became Yiddish also isn't clear. Rabbi Shlomo Yitzhaki, better known as the Rashi, studied in Worms two centuries before the Worms Mahzor was compiled. He or his disciples wrote glosses in Old French written in Hebrew characters, but what language Jews of that time would have spoken isn't clear.

The Worms synagogue was destroyed in Kristallnacht in 1938, ending centuries of the mahzor's use on Jewish holidays. But the mahzor and a trove of other Jewish manuscripts were spared thanks to "the vigilance of the municipal archive manager - a non-Jew - who attached the collection to the municipal archive with the rise of Hitler to power," a 1957 account in the Hebrew newspaper Kol Ha'am reported. But the archivist didn't want to let the Jewish books go, and only after courts ruled in favor of the Jewish petitions did the Worms collection, the mahzor included, make its way to Israel.

Since its delivery to Israel's National Library in 1957, the Worms Mazor has only been displayed publicly only a few times, most recently in 1985.

An Illumination from the Worms Mahzor: Description and Iconographical Study.
Bezalel Narkiss and Aliza Cohen-Mushlin

IN CONCLUSION

"Zol zayn tsum gutn. Far brokhe un hatslokhe. Far lebn un gesunt zayn. In a guter un mazl diker sho-zol zayn mit glik, lekhayim. It should all be good. To blessing and success. To life and health, in a good and lucky hour. It should be with happiness, to life."

Fiddler on the Roof

ABOUT THE AUTHOR

In her 76th year, totally new to the world of book writing, Barbara Rogers Jolovitz wrote *Reminiscences and Recipes* (North Country Press, 2012) which was entered in the 2013 Maine Literary Awards in the "John N. Cole Award for Maine-Themed Nonfiction." She collaborated with Ken Walsh, CEO of the Alfond Youth Center in Waterville, Maine, on *Behold the Turtle* (North Country Press, 2014). *"Turtle"* is the history of YMCA Camp Tracy, founded by her late husband Lester and two other Waterville men, and is written in the voice of the turtle. *A Singular Peluche* (North Country Press, 2014) is a fantasy about a teddy bear she found in a Goodwill toy bin waiting to be picked up and loved. *Fields of Dreams* (North Country Press, 2017) - Wrigley and Fenway are the fields – was co-written with Ken. It includes baseball going back to 1914, Code Talkers, curses, Hall of Famers, baseball on Iwo Jima, and on to the 2016 Chicago Cubs winning the pennant, and Waterville youngsters playing baseball at Purnell Wrigley Field in Waterville and Maine's Fenway at Camp Tracy. Barbara looks forward to the Major 60 Cal Ripkin World Series 2022 being played at both fields.

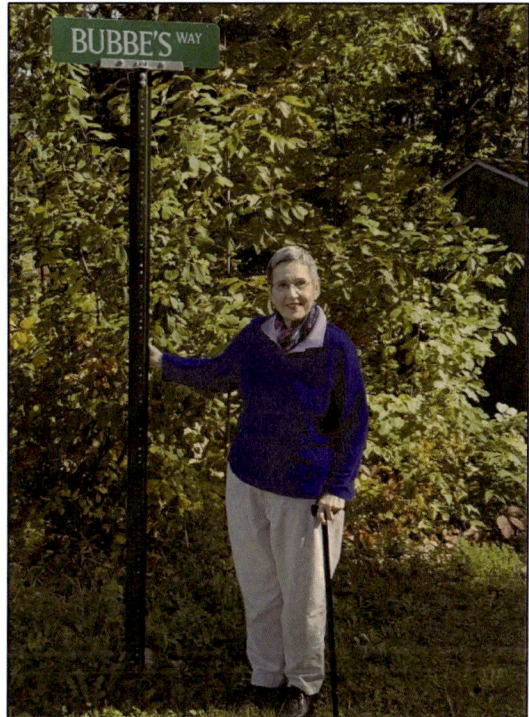

Street sign at YMCA's Camp Tracy. A gift from AYCC's Ken and Felicia.

Barbara's family includes children Karl and Deborah, grandchildren Ben and Amy, great grandson Jonah and granddog Mishka; Will and Austyn and granddog Barney; Nicky, Madison and Bubbe's World mishpocha.

www.ingramcontent.com/pod-product-compliance
Lightning Source LLC
Chambersburg PA
CBRC090821090426
42736CB00006B/240